FROM THE WINDOWS OF MY SOUL!

A Collective Work of Robert W. Evans (RWE)

ISBN
978-1-304-01685-0

TABLE OF CONTENTS

The five categories represented in this compilation of writings are, (1) Protest writings, reflecting the journey of a young black man growing up in America from the sixties until now. (2) Writing and Psalms unto God. (3) Children's Inspirational (4) Suffering In Silence. 5.) Love poems and song lyrics from published and unpublished compositions.

Preface

As a young black man growing up in the sixties and seventies afforded me the opportunity to internalize through direct experience the systemic racial inequalities permeating throughout our society in America.

Back then, the manifestation of the civil rights struggle to knock down the walls in America against racial inequality, systematic discrimination policies, and racial disparities by the mid-sixties, were in full bloom.

The majority of the young brothers and sisters we'd meet on the streets all professed to be writers. We'd say, "Hey man, long time no see… what have you been doing?" Most would respond, "Hey man, I've been busy writing… that's what I do now." We'd all say to one another, as we passed a joint around during socialization among one another.

During that period, I was able to have a one on one sit down with the great R & B legend, Jerry Butler. After reviewing some of my pieces he responded, "You know, you kind of remind me of a very near and dear friend of mine—Curtis Mayfield." That was then and remains to date the most absolute compliment I could and will ever receive. Curtis was then and continues to be today one of my most inspirational songwriter/composers.

Less than a year later, I found myself sitting down with the legendary songwriter. After reading a few of my pieces Curtis suggested that either I pick up an instrument to put my poems and writings to music, or partner with a musician… either way he suggested that I should definitely continue with my writing career. There are a couple of pieces in this book that Curtis Mayfield actually gave structural positive critique to. "World Power" and "Saying Something and Doing Nothing" being among them.

About a year later a member of the Sacred Hearts Catholic Diocese reviewed some of my writings by chance. She introduced my work to one of the Fathers there. Long story short… the Richmond Diocese sponsored my trip to New York where I had the opportunity to knock on doors and present some of my works.

When I returned home, they gifted me with a powder blue upright piano. I banged on it for a while, and then before I knew it, I was writing music.

The song "Colorless", which I'm dedicating to Sacred Hearts Diocese, was the first song I composed on my powder blue upright piano. It is therefore considered the mother of all of my music compositions.

Well for the past 25 years my writing has sustained me and has been the primary source of income for my livelihood. Back during the sixties and seventies I couldn't get my work published because of unabashedly mirroring the inherent racial biases, blatant bigotry and systematic intolerance I wrote about in my writings, that I not only witnessed here in America, but on many occasions as a strong outspoken young black man in America, was directly subjected to.

One of the main things Curtis insisted, as I continued to embark upon my writing career, was to always stay in charge of my creative works.

For the past 25 years I've been the owner/publisher and editor of my own newspaper, The Key Awareness newspaper here in Richmond, Virginia.

Based on all of the tragedies to people of color due to racism, bigotry and discrimination for the past 400 + years here in America… now is the time for voices against racial inequality and injustice in any form to stand firm and speak out. Plus, I own my own publishing business, so I don't need anybody's permission… especially those who continue to promote racial inequality, systematic racism, and who continues to operate from a premise and platform of social injustice against all people of color.

I hope my readers will find solace, some sense of peace and a more profound and mind opening understanding from reading "From The Windows of My Soul".

[#1] BLACK WINDS BLOW!

400 years, no trust,
400 years, still freedom's a must.
But times are changing by the hour
400 years of crumbling power.
We can see clearly now, yes we can,
now that the enlightened mind has awaken man

Still love for this land grows thin
while others control the wind
that blows life into our being.
True peace we'll find,
when black thoughts control black minds

Black Winds Blow!—Black Winds Blow!
I know, I know—Black Winds Blow!

The mothers of our women want
freedom from fears and taunts.
The sisters of our brothers want
peace from oppression's haunts

Yes, even when the storms of bigotry and hatred
attempts to blanket the earth, disguised as pure as the
whiteness of a winter's snow ,
the truth will always reveal through natural breezes
that Black Winds Blow!

System can you see our eyes,
tell us, what color is traumatize?
System, we know you realize,
that, like you, all we want is to stay alive
to get our own.
We've been black since our day of birth,
and measured with soul for what it's worth,

we're proud as hell right here on earth,
ain't goin' nowhere, gonna stay alert
to get our own—from our mother's home

Now fiction what some thought was fact,
the power to control the blacks;
A race who have struggled back
from the knowledge others thought we lacked

So take heed,
for one day all will feel the breeze,
then the world will know as we know,
That Black Winds Blow!

Written by Robert W. Evans (1968)

[#2] Intercessory Prayer: Somebody Prayed For Me!

"Take me from my cross...dip me into hell...still shall rise this unworthy soul to heaven...through Intercessory Prayer.
Lord, forgive us of our iniquities...our often diminished when challenged faith; for it is much too often we break Your heart...with our cold insensitive ways.
Lord, as You look upon Your children...and often see not promise of your intent, how greatly are we so out of place...mentioning the name of the one You sent?
Wrestle with the angel...if need be to intercede...this once lowly soul of ill repute...so thankful Somebody Prayed For Me.
Encamped amongst the demons...impious of Satan's lair...still, Godly angels set my spirit free...through Intercessory Prayer.
Despondent souls, tormented spirits, so wretched in despair...how blessed are we...the warriors You sent...for Intercessory Prayer.
How can we now claim...beyond our shame...a life of victory? Oh yeah, of the one You sent...tis your intent...that one did pray for me.
He died on the cross, to save my life...how worthwhile must I be? It surely can't be because of my worldly ways...thank God, Somebody Prayed for Me.
So hear my prayer O Lord...as I attempt to intercede...for those who are lost as I once was...before Somebody Prayed for Me.
So, take me from my cross, O Lord...and dip me, like Jesus into hell...still shall rise this unworthy soul to heaven...because of Intercessory Prayer.
Encourage our souls O Lord, to stay the course...tho waxed weary our souls to bare...blessed are we, the angels that weep and praise Your name...through Intercessory Prayer.
Hear the weeping O Lord, this day I pray...for tormented

souls loss in abysmal unfamiliarity. Remember O Lord... this one twas all but done...til Somebody Prayed for Me. I said, remember O Lord...this one twas all but done...til Somebody Prayed for Me. Now Your works I toil each day...unwavering faith dost I declare...a baptized soul in jubilation, thanks to Intercessory Prayer.
Thank God...Somebody Prayed For Me!
A psalm dedicated to my heavenly Father: [by, RWE] 5 / 28 / 2013.

[#3] What About The Children?

Every individual is the composer of his or her very own song to be sung in the key of life. Each song is unique in its own way. Some sing of happiness, some of sadness; some sing of love new and old; of dreams and aspirations. Some sing of life experiences good and bad, but, What About the Children? Shouldn't there be rhymes and rhythms in our repertoire of songs for the children? Shouldn't our wisdom reflect through our lyrics that we were once children too?

What about our music? Shouldn't the smiles of the children reflect upon our musical creativity a personal desire to produce beautiful melodies for the children that will ultimately be sung some day in concert by the children?

Let us never forget that all over the world little eyes are watching us, little ears are listening to us, little hearts have entrusted their well being with us, and little minds like tape recorders are taping us. So when we see them doing what they're doing, it's just their version of reflecting and interpreting the music of society.

Let us listen then to the natural sounds of the children before they start to copy and imitate our music.

You see, the song of a child is special. The heart of a child is pure. Their melodies are basic and simple; not filled with complicated orchestrations. If we take the time to listen to their lyrics, they simply say, "I Love You".

So, let us stop for a moment, take time out from our busy studio recording sessions in life of putting together our own songs and let the children concert us.

Let's let their little fingers play
let's let their little voices sing
let's celebrate them day by day
with joy only children bring/

Let's help them find the notes they need
and keep their lyrics strong
by strengthening their melodies
to keep beauty in their songs/

Let's let them sing their solo leads

but teach them duets too
let's keep their little minds at ease
by letting them know that... yes, we were once children too.

[#4] LOVE IS!

Your love is rainbow colors,
so gently illuminating my face.
You are all my lovers
floating out in space/

You keep floating from my arms,
like a puff of smoke you're gone/

Love lights all my fires,
love burns deep in me.
You can take me higher,
defy all gravity/

You can float me pass the clouds
where my rainbow loves all dwell,
settle me down inside your space
and love me tenderly/

Love is you,
you are love,

Settling in my soul,
like the love I dreamed I'd hold
so close to me,
so real to see,
so warm, you're heavenly/

Love is you,
you are love.

Your love, like the road,
entwines all paths of life.
You are all the beauty
of a sky bound bird in flight/

Please don't fly away from me,
like the road, your love's endlessly.

Travel me down your paths of life
and love me tenderly/

Love is you,
you are love/

[#5] BLACK MAN

YOU'RE SUCH A BEAUTIFUL CHILD!

You were brought to a foreign land,
by hateful oppressors.
Their evil ways you couldn't comprehend.

You were taught to pick cotton,
to tend the fields.
Your life was rotten,
oppressor's whip never yield.

You were a slave.
You were called boy 'til the day of your grave.

It's truly amazing how you survived.
Your families separated, women raped, your children brutalized.

But, Black Man, You're Such A Beautiful Child!
So much a beautiful child!

Believe not some others claim to have freed the slaves.
Through knowledge and education, perseverance and dedication, you're freeing yourselves
day by day.

A race as pure as the first morn in born.
As majestic in strength and beauty as a summer's sunrise.

Black Man, You're Such A Beautiful Child!

Captured kings and queens, dark prince and princess of pride,
continue your journey to the freedom side, because

Black Man, You're Such A Beautiful Child!

[#6] AMERICA—america!

You say, keep the black kids out of college,
keep the boogie in the streets.
We don't need interracial knowledge,
we don't need those rhythmic beats

You say, keep El Sanchez cross the border,
with those beans we dare not eat.
Hot tamales for a quarter,
we don't need no Mexi-treats.

AMERICA—america—what is this thing on me?
Why must I fight for equal rights,
from sea to shining sea?

AMERICA—America—what is this thing I see?
It's good for you when I pay dues,
and still cannot be free?

I say, keep those skin heads off my corner,
I don't want to crack those heads.
Scramblin hard this space I'm livin.
Tryin to stay alive, but livin every day afraid.

I believe in what I'm feelin.
Dream it real right from my head.
Believe my leaders in what they tell me.
Believe in every word they've said.

AMERICA—america—who is it foolin me?
When I must pay, but cannot stay,
equal to the free?

Walked the water, said Jesus did it.
Preached this land called liberty.
Believe in truth to be my leader,
but is there truth from you for me?

Believe in heaven inside me holy.
Believe the serpent's reality.
Believe in God, but holy heaven,
damn it's hell in poverty.

AMERICA—America—what is this thing on me?
Why must I fight for equal rights
from sea to shining sea?

AMERICA—America what is this thing on me?
Why must I fled in tormented dread of being killed, from sea to shining sea?

[#7] Let's Come Together People!

Our country is a human body,
the government is its brain.
Our country is a human body,
so rapidly going insane

Our country is a human body,
goodness is the heart.
Our country is a human body
that we are ripping apart.

Let's come together people—come together, yes we can.
Let's come together people—save the country—save the land.
Come together people—come together, I believe we can;
come together people—save our country—save our land.

If we take a look around we'll see—our country ain't my friend, what it claims to be.

The children are our flowers—they bloom throughout the world.
Racism and bigotry are learned behaviors —destroying impressionable minds of innocent boys and girls.

So, let's come together people—save our children, yes we can.
Let's come together people—save our country—save our land!
Written 1968.

[#8] Y'all Folks!

Wrong for me, but right for you, to do what you're telling
me not to do.
Don't believe I'm a whole being, got eyes for looking, but
not for seeing.
Jerking my pay, I keep working to stay above below.
Summer's fine when it's mine, but so seldom you know.
Still through it all I keep dancing to life's rhythms, missing
not a stroke,
of this funny, funny music from y'all folks!

[#9] YOU GOTTA BE CRAZY!

Born into this world, with life one.
With nobody else, no twin,
just my father's son.

One mouth to drink, one mind to think.
One soul to feel, and one love to give.

Now you want to capture my mind,
total my being, but,

You gotta be crazy—you gotta be crazy,
if you think you gonna take this away from me.

I'm living my only life, abiding by your laws.
Your holding me down ain't right…you with all your flaws.
We're living in just one world,
separated by your powers.
From 8 to 5 you suppress my mind,
now you're trying it after hours.

You gotta be crazy—you gotta be crazy,
if you think you gonna take this away from me.

Born into this world, with life one;
With nobody else…no twin,
just my mother's son.

One chance to be, myself and I to be free.
One dream I bring, the desire to do my thing.

You gotta be crazy—you gotta be crazy,

if you think you gonna take this away from me.

You Gotta Be Crazy!

Written By: Robert W. Evans
1975

[#10] SAIL ON BY!

All I wanna do is float along.
build my castle high in the sky,
capture my dream to make life a song,
let all my troubles just sail on by/

Sail on by—sail on by/

Fixin my woman snug under my arm,
ain't rappin nobody—ain't doin no harm,
if life can be easy—like to give it a try,
Just askin my troubles to sail on by/

Sail on by—sail on by/

Now I could be evil—make you let me be,
but then I'd be you—and I'm tryin to be me.
You've nothin to do but try and hold me down,
this time I'm telling you I don't want you around/ so

Sail on by—sail on by,
Just sail on by—sail on by/

Got me a melody,
gonna make me a tune.
Gonna sing about happy,
so that don't include you/

Seems like I've known you,
since short pants and lassie.
A million dreams and realities,
and you're still here harassin/

Now see—I could be evil and make you let me be,
but then I'd be you—but I've got to be me,
You've got nothin to do but try and hold me down,
this time I'm telling you trouble—I don't want you around/ so

Sail on by—sail on by,
Just sail on by—sail on by

Sail yourself free,

drift out pass the sea.
Go find yourself a storm,
won't mean a thing to me/

Sail yourself away,
to another space and zone.
Don't worry about a thing,
I'll tell them where you've gone/

Just sail on by—sail on by/

Cause all I wanna do is float along—build my castle high in the sky,
capture my dream to make life a song—let all my troubles just sail on by/
SAIL ON BY!

[11] A LETTER TO MY SON ON HIS 18TH BIRTHDAY: THE GIFT OF SPIRITUAL WISDOM

My son, I choose cautiously these words I say to you on this, your 18th birthday. As you seek to embark upon your journey into adulthood, understand that the direction you seek is not outward, it is within. Know that all roads begin and leadeth back to God. The road map to guide you successfully through your earthly journey, you will not find on a physical/ material plane, but through the portal of the spirit realm within.

So as you travel through this earthly plane, seek not to understand its meaning, but instead, if you journey within your spirit, you will learn your connections and your purpose unto God, and then the keys to worldly understanding will be given to you in intervals along your journey.

My son, I have shown you by example of how to endure all earthly attacks and still walk in spiritual strength with purpose. So fear not the attacks from those among you, for Satan will always send his sentinels to try to break your spirit, to stop your mission, which is to be a servant unto God.

Remember my son, as you continue through your earthly journey, "Greater is He that lives in you, than he that dwells in the world." It is by example that I have shown this to you, for even as of this writing I am under attack by Satan's sentinels, but they have no power, lest my Father gives it to them and that is not the purpose of our mission.

My son, I have always taught you that you have control over all things concerning you. Continue to learn self-control over your being. Let not your thoughts, or others' thoughts about you be a negative influence controlling your being. Go inside, dwell in the various rooms of your body house, familiarize yourself with the Godly oneness inside your spirit that gives you strength. Learn endurance, learn humility, learn patience, learn to forgive, be slow to anger, always help those in need, listen to that still small voice that tells you that you are your brother's keeper, wish only good for others, continue to be kind to all of God's creation, and always love yourself. As a matter of fact, love yourself, first.

And my son, as you continue your spiritual journey on this earthly plane and you embark upon the paths of others seeking to influence your travels in their direction, always remember upon encounters, "It is by their fruit, ye shall know them," in other words, beware of those around you whose trees never bear fruit as nourishment for the good of humanity.

So go on my son, on this your 18th birthday, embrace your journey, have no fear, and listen to that still small voice within, develop your being from within, for that is where the truth of your being lies. And remember my son; love yourself as I have loved you, and as your heavenly Father has loved you.

Happy Birthday!

From: Your Dad.

[#12] CHILDREN… ARE THE LIGHT FOR THE WORLD!

Children are the light for the world !
 Their laughter is the sun;
 Their little smiles brings warmth with the birth of each new day!

Children,
I like the children, pure, like cascading raindrops from heaven cleansing the earth.

In wealth,
Poverty,

Their little spirits radiates the brightness that lights the world.

When in darkness,
turn on the CHILDREN…

They are the light for the world!

By Robert W. Evans

[#13] CHILDREN HAND IN HAND!

Just children in a world
can show us,
how to understand the meaning of love

Playing hand in hand,
no colors to the man,
fun and love for all
is their code throughout the land

Children hand in hand—show God's love throughout the land
walking, talking, singing their song,
of a love so strong it'll never go wrong/

People looking on not
understanding all,
run from fears and doubts
so afraid of reaching out/

People have their ways of
covering up the truth,
keeping love within
afraid to turn it loose/

But children hand in hand—show God's love throughout the
land
Just walking, talking, singing the same song,
of a love so strong it'll never go wrong/

I pray some day I'll see this
world inside of me,
A world of harmony
where the soul of man is
free/

The poetry of my mind are
filled with poems of
sorrow,
Poems of love lost days,
love needed for tomorrow/

but Children hand in hand—show God's love throughout the
land
Walking, talking, singing their song,
of a love so strong it'll never go wrong/

I pray some day I'll see this
world inside of me,
A world of harmony
where the soul of man is
free/

The poetry of my mind
are filled with poems of
sorrow,
Poems of love lost days,
love needed for tomorrow/

But children hand in hand—show God's love throughout the
land/
Walking, talking, singing God's song,
of a love so strong it'll never go wrong!
[3rd song written on my powder blue upright piano--1970]

[#14] Pray Somebody's Gonna Care!

Believe my friend, what you feel you will,
but there's a test now being applied
for races to survive
and it's so very real.
All played up in classes, is a struggle for the masses.
You see it every day,
it comes around your way,
and its oh, so very clear.

So, if you can't get to the mountain top,
then you better help somebody there,
and if you're sure you can't make it,
Pray—Somebody's Gonna Care!

You see, there's a meeting about your being,
going on right here and now.
While you boogie to the woogie,
some serious thoughts are going down.

You say "naw—those people don't know me,
can't play nothin' on my mind".
But ain't man nor beast around today,
who can't be played on with time.

So, if you can't get to the mountain top,
then you better help somebody there,
and if you're sure you can't make it,
Pray—Somebody's Gonna Care!

You can be as wicked as a thought,
but still you might be sold, and you could be bought.
You see, strengths measured only by the test,
solid's the foundation prepared for the quest.

Danger, can't be no stranger, flowing through your mind,
not in this day and time...

Four hundred years of this BS
is a hell of a sign.

So, if you can't get to the mountain top,
then you better help somebody there,
and if you're sure you can't make it…
Pray—Somebody's Gonna Care!

But why can't you get there?
Written By: Robert W. Evans (1985)

[#15] NOWHERE!

They were speaking, but no one was listening, and through their utterances, still silence spoke their words/
The militants were coming, the hippies were strumming, while politicians were tossing their curves/

The world was a fair… everyone was there… the man was taking the tickets for the ride to nowhere—nowhere—nowhere

They were teaching, but no one was learning.
I was looking but not seeing a thing.
The sun was rising in my head. The people,
shapeless… their smiles, faceless… and the day seemed dreary and dread/

Somehow I could tell, we were all in a world, headed to the top—the top of nowhere—nowhere—no where

All my brothers and sisters look—ah look.
All my brothers and sisters, look at the weapons, the pistols, and wonder if the systems gonna miss us.
We've got a thing, and they just can't seem to resist us/

All my brothers and sisters, look, over here over there.
All my brothers and sisters, is this the ride to nowhere?/

The world was a fair, with everybody there… the man was taking the tickets for the ride to nowhere—nowhere—nowhere!

The veil of Racism won't allow you to see me. This shroud of Anger won't allow me to trust you
on this ride to nowhere… nowhere... nowhere!

1969

[#16] SUICIDE!

[Suffering In Silence]

Who weighs the soil life's
rains subside,
that wash into my river tides,
flood the land I abide,
and drowns my being in
suicide?/

SUICIDE

Through tainted smiles that
should not be,
watered eyes of misery,
uncertain hands that dare not
grasp
the perfect me in photographs/

Too many corridors of my
mind
to claim my dreams in lost and
found,
So afraid to say "hell no"
to the love that stunts my
growth/

Who weighs the soil life's
rains subside,
that wash into my river tides,
flood the land I abide,
and drowns my being in
suicide?/

When dares become afraid to
try,
though all is fair and still I cry,
Life becomes a pass me by
left in a corner with suicide/

Who cares to hear of what I
say
when stronger things have
washed away,
than me and my charades I
play
to strike the band another day/

When the perfect score as
though it seems,
twist in reality, destroy my
dreams,
brings the tears so to my eyes,
makes all things seem suicide/

Child of pretty I dared not be
to have one thought so spent
on me,
One fantasy—reality,
reality—a fantasy/

Knock me down and if I fall
the spiral envelops my all and
all,
Cry out loud for what it's
worth,
Cry out loud seems since my
birth/

The spiral entwine thus twists
my blend,
confuses myself way down
within,
No one will stay forever by my
side,
for who truly knows the
movement of suicide?/

[#17] DON'T YOU LET GO!
[Suffering In Silence]

Sure some tries in life might fell,
True you'll draw nothing from an empty well,
Fantasies from childhood dreams somehow don't seem as so,
but still, Don't You Let Go!
Don't You Let Go!

Sometimes rain falls in the midst of your fondest dreams,
and often winter stays too long it seems.
When you're tired stay and rest in the womb of my love for you.
Stay and rest until you're strong again to do what you feel you
need to do/

Don't You Let Go!

When days are dark, remember the sunshine,
remember, things worth having comes through dues with time.
Believe you are divine makings of your spiritual maker,
for special reasons you breathe the breath of your creator/

Don't You Let Go!

Ain't no loser when all out is tried.
Failure is not, not being first, it's the giving up inside.
I believe in you, what you do always…
In your life's ups and downs, I'll forever stay/

Don't You Let Go!

Lift your head to the sky,
Spread your wings and fly,
Give it one more try,
You will succeed by and by/

Believe in that feeling you feel deep inside.

Believe if it can be done it can be done by you.
Believe, when you believe, you can't lose,
and then believe that I believe in you too/

Don't You Let Go!

[#18] I'M STILL ME!

I lived my life
In the realm
of good
I'm sure/

From the pain
of loneliness
you send me
money to cure/

I'M STILL ME!

You say time
has wedged the brace
to separate me
from the youthful wall/

You think because
you've reached the age
of thirty three
you know it all/

I'M STILL ME!

And now in my twilight
I can't lift
a hundred pounds
over my head/

Is that any reason
to label me
incapable,
dead/ the truth is I never could.
I'M STILL ME!

Through world wars
I've been,
In strength
my weakness cried/

In life I've fallen
so deeply down,
even now, but still I pick
myself up
and try/cause,
I'M STILL ME!

I've seen empires tumble,
I've seen dynasties crumble,
I've watched helplessly

love taken away/

Tho a million dreams have
shattered
through the pieces I've
gathered
enough insight to
make a day/

I'M STILL ME!

Although your system don't
seem to include me
in this
worldly survival,

But I was dealing,
making plans to maintain
for me, for you
long before your arrival/

I'M STILL ME!

Herd the likes
of me
all up in one
small space

allow my knowledge,

my family roots
to just dissipate/

I'M STILL ME!

You think time
has wedged the brace
to separate me from
the useful wall.

You think because
I've reached the age of seventy
three
I'm about to fall.hey,/

I'M STILL ME!

From child, to youth, to adult,
to beautiful and knowledgeable
human being—GOT DAMN
IT

I'M STILL ME!

Written By: Robert W. Evans
1973

[#19] Yoyos, Elevators, Escalator Steps!

Yoyos, elevators, escalator steps,
Stock markets, Ferris wheels, notches in a belt

Rating polls, fickle souls, monetary wealth,
Life's included, you can't exclude it, it blends in with the rest

They all have their ups and downs, downs and ups
ups and downs and ups

So when life seem to reach its all time low,
Just remember,

Yoyos, elevators, escalator steps, stock markets, Ferris wheels, notches in a belt, rating polls, fickle souls, monetary wealth; yes, life's included, you can't exclude it cause it fits in with the rest.

Those Yoyos, Elevators and Escalator Steps!

[#20] SMILE!

A smile is the brightest thing
to lighten your darkest day,
A smile can change the rain
to dew drops of marmalade/

A smile is as pretty
as life's prettiest picture,
I just love it when you smile
because a smile surely fits ya/

There's nothin I'd rather see
more than you smile at me,
It's sort of a mental thing
that causes my heart to sing/

A smile is as lovely
as the loveliest of lovely,
A smile is as warm
as bread in mama's oven/

Keep on smiling… I just love it
when you smile… especially
when you're smiling at me!

[#21] TIME!

5 years, fun life brings,
Playgrounds, schools, swings and things

10 years, sure was swell,
learning how to be aware
of what friendships are all about,
never knowing of fears or doubts.

15 years, such beautiful times,
learning the meaning of life's rhymes,
Ball, music, fun and games,
digging on girls calling my name.

20 years, I see the change,
playing life's a much serious game.
Standing up and falling down a lot,
picking myself up off the ground a lot,
reaching out for a hand to touch.
Finding my woman I love so much.

25 years have come and gone,
sometimes I want to turn and run back home.
But yesterday is but a gone tomorrow,
filled with traces of laughter and moments of sorrow.

Too fast we travel through the cycles of life,
as if riding on jet propelled wings…
But every now and then, let us remember to, on occasion, to just
glance back and smile… as we continue our journey forward…
For who knows what the future brings!

[#22] WE ARE ONE... GOD IS THE SOURCE OF OUR SUPPLY!

If we accept the truth of our being, that we are not physical beings seeking a deeper understanding of our spiritual connection with God; but instead, know that we are spiritual entities, one with God who dwells in the temple of our souls, the source of All Creation, the catalyst of our energy while we dwell on this physical plane, we will then live a more purposeful, a more fulfilled and fearless life throughout our earthly journey.

God is not there hiding somewhere in the stratosphere, where if we're lucky, we might for a fleeting moment receive an abstract and vague epiphany of our purpose and connection with Him. No, He is where He has always been, right here in the souls of our being, waiting for us to receive the knowledge of this truth.

Know that we are one with the Creation of All; therefore, are a part of all creation. Accepting this truth of our oneness with God, know that we carry the answers to the mysteries of the universe within the temple of our inner-being; the same temple within where The Spirit of The Living God dwells. Jesus said, "As the sun-beam is one with the sun; I and my Father are one." There is not us, and all of our daily earthly stuff, and our day to day earthly foolishness a part from God, who sees all and knows all. There is only God: omniscient, omnipotent and omnipresent. We Are One--- God is the Source of Our Supply!

There is not God separate from us, where on Sundays and maybe on Wednesday nights, we do our weekly ritual of including God in our lives to magically balance our weekly life accounts, or maybe pray to Him to become our spiritual 'wonder pill' as an instant 'cure-all' for our pains and our sufferings, which in many cases are brought on by our spiritual disobedience and slothfulness to start with.

There is always God in our presence; No--- there is always us in God's presence. He is the sun--- we are the sun-beams. He sends us out as rays of sunshine to touch and bring to light those who are loss and shrouded in darkness. Jesus said:

"Let your light so shine before men, that they may see your good works, and glorify your Father which is in heaven."

If at this precise moment, we touch and agree that We Are One--- and that God Is The Source of Our Supply, instantly the knowledge of this truth will set us free. Once we accept and understand the Truth of Our Being, that God is not out there somewhere floating on a magical spiritual cloud waiting to scoop us up; but instead, is right here by our sides, in our souls, in all that we are, we will then set the captive spirit free. Free to receive our spiritual gifts, abundantly.

Know that everywhere we take ourselves, we take God. We are an extension of His presence. As the cord is an extension of its energy source, the conduit that supply the dwelling with electrical energy bringing forth illumination and life; we are one with our Energy Source. God is our energy supply, our Illumination.

As I stated earlier, this spiritual understanding will bring us a more purposeful, a more fulfilled and fear free life as we continue our earthly journey. Even though we are born physically on this earthly plane, shrouded in man-made fear, man's weaknesses and fears do not control the Truth of Our Being… which is to be in the world—but not of it.

Fear has controlled man since the beginning of time, thus limiting and robbing man of his spiritual gifts and abilities, causing him to operate in lack, sickness, ignorance, and disease. But, because we are born into a mesmeric, hypnotic state of being, does not mean that that is who we are. We are children of God's, His sons and daughters, with all of the God given talents, gifts and earthly endowments given to Jesus. We are greater than the earthly powers of this hypnotic state of being. Jesus said, "In all things be thou perfect like Me." He also said, "Greater works than these, Ye can do."

To operate in the knowledge of our oneness with God is to operate in a world without fear. To operate on a perfect plane is to operate in total faith. In faith there is no fear--- fear is the absence of faith. Know today, that In God We Are One--- God Is The Source of All of Our Supply.

I humbly greet you and thank you for reading this message. (Source RWE).

[#23] OF ALL THAT I AM / GOD IS!

God is the Creator of all things beautiful,
All roads in life leadeth from and travel back to God,
God encompasses all.

All that has to do with it is of God.
All that has to do with it is from love, of love, in love.
Peace, harmony, understanding, emotions, sensitivities,
compassion, love for humanity
are so derived of God .

God is the creator and everlasting of all things beautiful;
and we being of His creation, in the spirit realm,
we too are love infinity.

The physical body is but a vehicle to transport, mobilize,
that which is real, through the portal of the spirit being.

Go beyond, go inside, when we were given the gift of life we
were automatically given the gift of God.

And in that spiritual concept, when the physical being ceases,
and we become one with God- We shall live eternally.

Just as the living memories of our loved ones will dwell in our
spirits forever!

In memory of
Aunt Arlene

By Robert Evans
(RWE)

[#24] Just The Price We Pay For The Space We Occupy!

In conversations—don't care to rap,
Shoving laws—I don't intend to heed,
Wasting too much precious time washing off crap
others insist on putting on me

Spent a lifetime so far,
as of now stop pretending,
If we don't listen to one another… you and I,
there's no sign in sight of ever mending,

But if one should fall
we both might cry, cause
It's just the price we pay
for the space we occupy!

We're here together,
I'd prefer alone,
You built the ships
took me away from home.

Ain't no peace from your beast of prejudice.
Better make it right, you can't make me white, and I bet you this,
without me here, what a struggle to survive,
It's just the price we pay for the space we occupy!

Spent a lifetime in my living mind
of trying to be free,
Ain't no way you can ever repay
what it is costing me.

Don't ask for much, it's just as such
of a mind in understanding,
that there's a new me arriving, with all intent of surviving
and so awesome in demanding.

I said, don't ask for much, it's just as such

of a mind in understanding,
that there's a new me arriving, with all intent of surviving
and so awesome in demanding.

Down now but, up, don't be surprised,
It's just the price we pay for the space we occupy!

Putting your knee on my neck, I just can't see
when we both know it won't fit.
Negative suppression causes the same in aggression,
equal only to bull---t/ who needs it?

My father, creator of me, I feel your time well spent,
carry I will the torch of freedom for equality so meant.

Ain't nothing new, just what I do for races to survive,
It's just the price we pay for the space we occupy!

Ain't no livin child I bare without the need inside for me to care
for them to be free.
Ain't no life I live, ain't no love for me to give, without true
knowledge
of self—ain't no other way to be---but free.

Through time it's proven—of strength selected—so chosen, to
lead.
Through the womb of life so travel—the sperm of true unravel—
a new breed,
Free—no other way to be—but free.

It's just the price we pay for the space we occupy!
Written By: Robert W. Evans
1970

[#25] SAYING SOMETHING/ DOING NOTHING!

People over there are saying something
People over here are doing nothing
Just saying something and doing nothing/

To the wars the people sigh
To the hunger the babies cry
Some old people wishing to die
while young folks getting high/

Hitler's back, dressed in black
rapping to the haves about the have nots
of how his bag is so intact/

Still you and I, a lot of soul
tripping on life, while we're growing old
Helping the man keep the cat up the pole
by pimping our women on welfare dough/

People over there are saying something
People over here are doing nothing
Just saying something and doing nothing/

A brother O.D.ed yesterday
I know, I saw the man take his body away
and all the time the man's digging the fade
hoping to make everybody a lighter shade
while we're breaking our backs for the bills to be payed
the man's pushing us down until we've laid and laid/

People over there are saying something
People over here are doing nothing
Just saying something and doing nothing/

Killing our brothers, raping our daughters
drinking from the fountains of polluted waters
talking about ain't instead of oughta/

But if we just get up off our sides
we can bring unity together with pride
to cease the beast of burden who thrive
among love, our favorite child,
I said among love, our favorite child/
Instead of saying something and doing nothing,

Just saying something and doing nothing,
Saying something and doing nothing!

By Robert W. Evans
1976

[#26] REMEMBER THE MISSION IS OURS BUT THE MINISTRY BEONGS TO GOD…SO IT CAN NEVER FAIL!

Having difficulty fulfilling your earthly-Godly assignment? Well here are a few tips that may assist you in your daily ministry. First, "know that the mission is ours… but the ministry belongs to God… so it can never fail."

Also, we must believe that although we are operating on an earthly-worldly plane… still we are not from this earthly-worldly sphere… *"We have not received the spirit of the world but the spirit who is from God, that we may understand what God has freely given us."* [Corinthians 2:12].

Know that unto each blessed soul, that God has blessed us with a direct relationship with Him… and with our own personalized ministry to serve Him. The opportunity to serve God, we should treasure and serve Him in total faith with all of our heart and soul. Jesus said: *"For where your treasure is there will your heart be also."* [Matthew 6:21]. But in order to serve successfully we must first surrender our earthly-worldly ways of thinking and being. We must not be afraid to release to the winds of change, our worldly fears… to toss into the sea of forgiveness wrongs that others have done to us… and we to them… and to keep our portals of humility open so that our channels of receptivity can remain free flowing to receive purely and clearly our Godly assignments.

For it is through the portals of forgiveness and humility that we grow spiritually. Also, remember: never get so caught up in the characters of those whom God has placed in your immediate space to be blessed by your service. Keep in mind that it does not matter to God how we feel about those whom He has placed in our path to be a blessing to through our services, nor how they feel personally about us. Know that this is His ministry, and that we are serving Him… not the people in front of us. Remember: *"Answer not a fool unto his folly… lest thou also be like unto him."* [Proverbs 26-4].

So always remain focused on the purpose of the mission and not on the characters involved in the assignment. Stay focused on your Godly instructions and never take the assignments personally. We must practice daily, learning to keep our emotions out of our assignments… for the attacks on our emotions will surely come… as certain as the sun ushers in the light of each new day… as certain as like a shroud, darkness covers night… many will seek to destroy the temple housing the soul of our Godly ministry. But we must remain girded in faith and in belief that: *"Our enemies will be clothed in shame, and the tents of the wicked will be no more."* [Job 8:22].

"For the Lord will grant that the enemies who rise up against you will be defeated before you. They will come at you from one direction but flee from you in seven." [Deuteronomy 20:4].

So my beautiful brothers… my beautiful sisters as we continue our earthly-worldly sojourn carrying out our Father's assignment… remember that it is His bidding not ours that we're seeking to accomplish… so let us be mindful always that "Greater is He that lives in us, than he that dwells in the world." And that we must stay girded always with the armor of faith, trust, humility, forgiveness, charity, compassion, understanding, love, and spiritual obedience remembering always that "The Mission Is Ours… But The Ministry Belongs To God… So It Can Never Fail."

And one more reminder… never forget to take the time out to enjoy and celebrate life… for it is indeed a precious gift from God. So in our worldly travel let our actions speak for us… let our joy for life be a reflection of God's universal love for humanity.

Let our disciplines and obedience exemplify that we are one with our Creator… and that the abundance of love, peace and joy manifested within, be amplified and abound worldly. So my beautiful brothers and sisters, I encourage and beseech you to first love God… then yourselves, and then those in the world to whom we have been instructed to assist.

Jesus said, *"I have told you these things, so that in Me you may have peace. In this world you will have trouble. But take heart! I have overcome the world."* [John 16:33].

"For just as the suffering of Christ flow over into our lives, so also through Christ our comfort overflows." [2 Corinthians 1:5].

So let us remember always… especially on occasion, when the light of our spirits dim, and our souls wax weary from the journey… that, "Although the Mission is Ours… The Ministry Belongs To God… So It Can Never Fail."

Stay girded, Stay Strong, Stay Blessed, and Stay the Course. [R.W.E.]

[#27] Self's Place!

Everyone must take the trip
through mind, to heart, to soul,
journey down the streets of self, within,
only you can go/

People you meet on different streets
are unalike as sun and moon,
but when put together—like natures weather
creates a beautiful you/

Self's Place—where all life's mysteries communicate
Self's Place—where spiritual harmony originates.

From whence you fled within—you must tread again
while the stream of life is flowing,
for you must conquer then—the beast who lurks within
the rivers of unbeknowing/

You see, it's nature's way to make the weak a self made slave
to the changes he fear inside,
but belief in self—is the greatest wealth,
it's universal pride/

Self's Place—where all life's mysteries communicate
Self's Place—where spiritual harmony originates/

Written By: Robert W. Evans

[#28] FORGIVENESS!

Wish not vengeance on those who seek to persecute or harm you. Instead look through the soul of man and there you will find the spirit of God. "Vengeance is mine sayest the Lord." "Judge not lest ye be judged." Understand that we are all God's children. Always remember, a misguided soul falls privy to the work of the devil. Stay on the path of righteousness though it is straight and narrow.

When forgiving others seek forgiveness of yourself also. There is but one perfect one. When we forgive, it sets the spirit free from negative bondage. It releases healthy cells throughout the brain and body of the forgiver. Like milk, forgiveness does a body good.

As you continue to do God's will, know that you are in the world of flesh but not of that world. The real world flows through the portal of the God realm; the spirit world.

Forgive those who seek to harm you whether it is by physical might or the wickedness of the tongue. Forgive them and remember, they can only see you according to the level or degree of their spiritual growth and understanding. So, look through the wickedness of man. Know that the carnal mind is kin to the devil. If you look deep enough into the soul of every man, you will find the spirit of God.

Forgive.

By Robert W. Evans

[#29] YOU'RE COMING THROUGH!

Youthful dreams create tunes, sing them to the wind/ melody realizations are yours/ like breezes float them afar/ pass the end the beginning lies/ believe in the light deep inside, deep in you/ don't be afraid of the dark tunnel, just know that you possess the light deep in your spirit, deep in your soul/
Don't quit the task before the test/ preparation, pain before pleasure/ that extra step, take it/ you can/ it is of you derived all things beautifully abound/

The system dictates/ in you lies the truth of your being/ believe you are… you are one… one part of all/ all things probable to self achievement universally be you/ all things spiritually you are so derived of, and of they, you/ blend/ harmony/ concordance/ harmonic components/ combined elements of you/ merge your steps/ conquer the dark/ develop mental light, from the light, sight/ yours/ deep within/ hidden/ must seek the depths to find/ follow the signs/ the answer only you can find/ learn the signs/ self belief, determination, dedication to well being, trust, pain before pleasure/ work hard/ dedication to beliefs/ the mind, body, the spirit/ listen/ through your years you can hear it/ everything in your life has been to be/ learn the lyrics, the melody's free/

When hot, jump into yourself/ refresh in your pool of cool/ go on high; on high, dive deep into your self/ surface/ breathe the breath of life/ no other way to be/ self/ free/

Cold/ truth can be cold/ only a feeling like hot/ strip it, whip it/ cold, gold only you can control/ experiences are wealth properly ascertained/ in you the meaning's clear/ like the sky/ reflections/ stars to you to stars/ go beyond sight/ go beyond self doubt/ belief/ believe in self/ wealth of untold dimensions/

Know that you are of all things/ so all things created of God are of you so derived/ all things conceivable flow through your filters/ believe you can/ you are/ you always were/ you always will be/ you are the light, a ray of hope/ you grow larger the closer you pursue your trek forward/ make the wishers move over, give you room, cause, (hey baby) You're Coming Through!

[#30] WHO GAVE AWAY MY RIGHTS?

Our leaves might be brown
but that's no reason for somebody trying to shake our family tree down.
We let green grow your grass,
can't you see our family tree's here to last.

Our roots grow deep down in the soul of mother earth.
Our tree blossoms fruit and the world has eaten its worth,
and you have too.

Leaves of our family tree a hundred shades brown.
Count them, count them, count them, a hundred shades beautiful brown,

So who gave away my rights?—Who gave away my rights?
Who gave away my rights?

Took away my father, separated my mother,
Killing my beautiful sons, raping my precious daughters,
Who gave away my rights?—Who gave away my rights?
Who gave away my rights?

My God living in me,
tells me the plants, animals, and I were created to be free.
This overwhelming hurt inside I feel,
to see my people having to live their one life under totalitarian will.

We've all been given the gift
of one life, one love to give.
A world as beautiful as ours
should be a Utopia for all to live,
and you know it's true.

So who gave away my rights?—Who gave away my rights?
Who gave away my rights?

Took away my father, separated my mother,
killing my strong sons, raping my beautiful daughters,

Who gave away my rights?—Who gave away my rights?
Who gave away my rights?

Took me from my land, took my land from me, killed my dog
and cat, separated all my kin!

Who gave away my rights?—Who gave away my rights?
Who gave away my rights?

IT SHO WASN'T ME!!!

Robert
W. Evans
(1970)

[#31] POLLUTION!

You know, I feel we should all come together
to strengthen the brotherhood,
put a hold on pollution
like we should.

It's tragic when love gives way to hate.
When wars determine fate.
When the rich for granted squanders.
When life gives way to hunger.

Preaching us false hope----------------- pollution
Streets are filled with dope------------- pollution
Chemicals in our water----------------- pollution
Ain't livin like we oughta------------- pollution

Pollution---------------- pollution

People in our world saying how much they care
about the welfare of all mankind.
But tell me how in the hell if everybody cares
the world's in such a bind.

Now I ain't perfect and neither are you,
but we both profess to see the light.
I think it's wrong to go along,
if the movement just don't seem right.

I see pollution---- I see pollution---- everywhere

Polluted air so thick it's getting hard to breathe,
corruption in the air keeps on choking me,
weakening the pillars of our society.

I see pollution—I see pollution—everywhere

Polluted minds so infested from the greed,

together we can save them for our children's needs.
Together we can cleanse our polluted seas, of pollution.

When love gives way to hate… Pollution
When wars determine fate… Pollution
When the rich for granted squanders… Pollution
When life gives way to hunger… Pollution

Pollution everywhere!
[but thank God for the young people… I see you, and proud of you]

[#32] I PRAY!

I have to pray, pray, I have to pray, pray!
Sometimes I bend, sometimes I cry.
Sometimes life's winds try and blow me by,
but I keep holding on no matter come what may,
my God lives in my soul and I know how to pray.

Sometimes life seems so hard and so unfair.
I need but to go inside, cause He's always there.
He feeds me when I'm hungry, warms me when I'm cold,
He eases all my burdens, He lightens my every load.

And I pray for the homeless sleeping in the streets,
I pray for the children who don't have enough to eat.
I pray for the missing children to come home,
I pray the molesters just leave the kids alone.

I pray that the wicked would see the Christ light.
The light to guide us through storms and dark of night.
The light to turn on whenever you are down,
keeps your head above water, your feet on solid ground.

I know my Father loves me, His will I pray be done.
He cleansed my soul with love, He gave His only Son.
He comforts me in sorrow, blesses every need.
I pray throughout life's travels my Lord in me is pleased.

I pray for the homeless sleeping in the streets,
I pray for the children who don't have enough to eat.
I pray for an end to human degradation.
For peace love of Jesus supreme in every nation.

I pray for the sinners, I pray for the weak.
I pray for the strong to protect the meek.
I pray for a drug free society,
for harmony and peace, for all humanity.

I pray for an end to wars and rumors of.

I pray all preachers are teaching how to love.
I pray for an end to world prejudice,
with Jesus in our hearts, these things will not exist.

I pray to the God who answers my prayers… I pray, I pray, I pray!

By Robert W. Evans

[#33} For the Children With Hunger Near!

Christmas Eve sure is swell,
mistletoe, that turkey smell.
For the child who's got it all,
on Christmas Day gonna have a ball.

Oh, but for the child with hunger near,
Christmas's just another day of the year.
He can't smile but sheds a tear,
cause it's Christmas time and he's tryin to live.

Christmas comes but once a year,
everybody is tryin to give,
but for the child with hunger near
it's Christmas time and he's tryin to live.

You and I, the lucky ones,
Christmas to us a lot of fun.
See the toys for the boys and girls,
sing of joy throughout the world.

Oh, but for the child who's never seen,
Santa Clause or a Christmas dream.
Never sung of the first noel,
or all is calm all is well,
is the child we need to share,
the Christmas spirit with everywhere.

He's the child who sheds a tear.
He's the child with hunger near.

Got my Christmas, so have you,
feel I'm singing of the majority too,
but somewhere there's a child who's never known,
for the Christmas spirit has never been shown.

He's the child that sheds a tear,

never smiles or had a cheer,
now it's Christmas time and he's tryin to live.
You see, He's the Child with Hunger Near!

Please help!

[#34] MAMA!

Mama strive,
7 to 4
she worked so hard,
Took care of five,
heaven knows
she played her part/

Never won an Oscar,
received no Emmy
for the roles she played.
Kept our bellies filled on
food,
and full of wood
that wood stove stayed/

Believe through my years,
Mama to be an angel,
so I know love, when it's
love,
it's no stranger/

Been with me through my
years
all the time.
Ain't no lovin like lovin
that sweet Mama of mine/

Expressions of Mama,
tears choke up in my soul,
Cross my mind Mama,
love automatically unfolds/

Mama you've always been
to me
the love blending all
seasons,
In this chaotic world, I look
to you, I see reasons (love)/

The love you've shown me
I've captured, reciprocated,
it's mine,

Just hope to be able to share
that kind of love,
in my life time/

You see mama, through you
I've learned the meaning of
life,
So tested my strength,
sacrificed/

I'll just go on being,
just go on seeing through
love you're showing me/

Got a good woman Mama,
love so true,
Inner beauty and love
like you/

Mama, you've given up
youth
I can attest,
I've seen youthful years go
by
raising us at your best/

Mama, I love you,
everybody loves you

just for what you do/

Ain't trying to be no poet,
just love you Mama and
hope you know it/

I'm saying what my spirit
feels,
Just setting here writing
about one of the few things
real/

Love you Mama,
through childhood you see,
hope someday I'll be the
son
You felt I'd be/
LOVE
HAPPY BIRTHDAY
Mama!

[#35] WHY DON'T WE TAKE A DAY?

I believe we hold the key
to wars or peace.
Through harmony we can sing a melody of life.
A melody's alright,
when it's sung for all humanity…
for all of you and me.

So Why Don't We Take A Day—try it a brand-new way—why?
Why Don't We Take A Day—forget to discriminate--why?

Can't believe all's not meant to be free,
like clouds above my head.
Like a bird to fly away.
Like life sustaining rays of a sunny day!

Why Don't We Take A Day—try it a brand-new way—why?
Why Don't We Take A Day—forget to discriminate—why?

We're taking away all of life's beauty,
We're taking away all of life's beauty.

Loving wishes,
replaces prejudices…
A world of love for all mankind!

Love's not missin.
It's just so deeply hidden,
within the recesses of our minds.
So many times our God has shown us the signs, so,

Why Don't We Take A Day—try it a brand-new way—why?

Why Don't We Take A Day—forget to discriminate—why?

Robert W. Evans

[#36] World Power!

Dialectical materialism, open mindedness, peace or truth,
all mere idiosyncrasies from a nation steeped in abuse.
Destruction to all minority groups, red, yellow
tan, me and you/

World Power at any cost,
World Power to this nation a must.
World Power at any cost,
World Power, who'll take the loss?

Success you claim to find.
While success, all the time,
you're killing the beautiful brothers and sisters of mine/

World Power, World Power,
keep killing every hour, a mother's loving flower.
World Power, World Power,
your destruction keeps turning
the sweet to sour/

But World Power, when you finish killing… will there be any world left for those
whom peace is willing?
World Power, it shouldn't matter whether our skin is of black, brown or tan;
What idiot determined skin color to be the measure of a man?

Judge not lest ye be judged, whether coffee drinkers, pill poppers, crackheads or boozers,
without real change in thought… we are all losers.

World Power at any cost.
World Power to this nation a must.
World Power at any cost,
will your children or mine take the lost?

The thoughts in your mind, have been explained clearly by your crimes,

of the power you seek to find, while killing the beautiful brothers and sisters of mine.

World Power, World Power,
you're killing every hour,
a mother's loving flower.

World Power, World Power!
(Written 1968 by RWE)

[#37] COLORLESS!

If I could have a wish to come true
It would be that orange was green
and red was blue

Or pink was gold
and tan was gray
and the rays of love
shine its warmth on each new day

And man would accept man just as he is
and leave the hatred in yester—years
That's how it would be, in a world of Utopian harmony

And if lime was silver
or brown was yellow
and every man
was just another fellow

If purple was black
and black was white
then the wars of color
would vanish in the night
That's how it would be, in a world of Utopian harmony

If I could have a wish to come true
it would be that you could see me
and I could see you

And our bids for peace
would see us through
the hardships and strife
that so often plague me and you

But of all the things I wish
this one I wish the best
that all the prejudices of the world
were Colorless!

{written in 1970--first song written on my powder blue upright piano}

[#38] A LONG WAY FROM HOME/ HALF WAY TO HOPE!

Going to find my Hope—she's out there somewhere on the loose.
The devil stole her mind while we were searching for the truth.
I came down and turned around—now my life's a natural high.
My baby's mind—I'm trying to find—it's somewhere in the sky/
and I'm ,
A LONG WAY FROM HOME (but I'm half way to Hope) said I'm
A LONG WAY FROM HOME (but I'm half way to Hope)

We challenged life as it came—and played it like a game.
We took our chances just the same—now the devil's in Hope's veins.
I came down and turned around—now my life's a natural high,
but my baby's mind—I'm trying to find—it's somewhere in the sky/
and I'm,
A LONG WAY FROM HOME (but I'm half way to Hope)

Got to find that woman I love so very much.
I'm longing for her kisses and I'm needing for her touch.
But it's my fault my baby's gone—I got her strung out on a line,
now dope is in her arms—while the devil's in her mind/

I got to find my baby—just got to find and save her/
so I'm,

A LONG WAY FROM HOME (but I'm half way to Hope) said I'm,
A LONG WAY FROM HOME (but I'm half way to Hope)

Hope was so tender sweet, -- so naive to the street.
Knew nothing about nothing—and less about her me.

Such a beautiful child—with that universal smile,
would do anything she could—to fit into my style/

I had Hope a dealing in the streets,
at home in the kitchen she preferred to be,
I was too busy playing street games,
I couldn't see my Hope being swallowed by the change.

Now it's my fault my baby's gone—I got her strung out on a dime,
now dope flows through her arms—the devil flows through Hope's mind/

So I'm,
A LONG WAY FROM HOME (but I'm half way to Hope) said I'm,
A LONG WAY FROM HOME (but I'm half way to Hope)

Someday I'll find you Hope—I love you!

[#39] You Say Iran—I Say I Jogged

(Any Love Lost?)

Gas, higher than I've ever been,
America's going back.
Oil, warm my children crisis,
winter turns white, I'm still cold, and black.

Cost of living rises daily
cracking my skies.
Maintaining—barely,
tears behind my smiles.

Now you say Iran—I say I jogged (any love lost?)

You say Jesus walked the water,
I say cotton he bailed.
Now you say go to Iran,
I say go to hell, (any love lost?)

You live on the hill,
won't allow me to be.
Camouflage your movements,
fool society.

For the moment be strong,
fight, win,
but after the war
will we be unequal again?

Now you say Iran—I say I jogged (any love lost?)

Wish I could sell my meat,
the prices in the store.
Could build me a ship—steal some land,
in the name of explore.

Such prices of your fads,
all the while inflation's killing me.

How can I not say what's on my mind?
Huh—society?

Now you say Iran—I say I jogged (any love lost?)

Lost a lot, my brothers, wars one, two, Iraq,
Vietnam.
Another chess game to be played,
a sham.

Now you say Iran—I say I jogged (any love lost?)

Test of the devil
has come today,
no white saviors
coming my way.

What has been
is still here to be,
the struggle of my people,
for real equality.

You say Iran—I say I jogged.
I ask you again... is there any love lost?

You say to the eyes of the world,
a slap in the face.
I say over four hundred years ago,
that slap took its place.

Price of gas is going up again
I bet.
I'm lower middle class America,
but I feel I'll be walking yet.

Can't afford to work
without a yell.
Don't know much bout no heaven,
but an authority on hell

Now you say Iran—I say I jogged (any love lost?)

World war two
my father did.
Returned of troubled mind,
til the day he quit.

Wilma Rudolph, her heart out she ran,
representing the states.
Couldn't set down for a cheeseburger,
in good ole U.S. of A.

Now you've got nerve to say Iran,
well, I say I jogged (is there any love lost?)

Pray my soul
won't give in.
As a race
wouldn't be livin,

Genocide
so hard to bare…
but just one step below
your welfare.

Superman never saved me from attack.
Wonder woman, if only I could white my back.
Survival test me everyday society;

and now you say Iran—I say go to hell…
I'm going jogging!

Written By: Robert W. Evans

[#40] THROUGH TIME—OCEAN!

Through time the sweat and tears of life became the stream.
The stream, in its youth and vitality for life created the river.
The river of life flowed.
Through time, wisdom and love, the river branched, trickled down many
water ways, enhancing all creativity.
Through time the river continued to flow, pouring its gathered knowledge
of life into once empty and barren basins.
Through time the stream, the river, no longer in their youth, derived
the mighty majestic sea.
The sea in its magnificent splendor and infinite wisdom mated mother nature
to give birth to what is now an unceasing flow of life,
THE OCEAN.

It matters not whether we be the youthful stream, the river or the wise
majestic sea, we all have and will continue to merge and to flow always in support
of life's OCEAN!
Stay Blessed, Stay The Course…and Keep The Faith!
A glimpse "From The Windows of My Soul".
(by Robert W. Evans (RWE)

www.ingramcontent.com/pod-product-compliance
Ingram Content Group UK Ltd.
Pitfield, Milton Keynes, MK11 3LW, UK
UKHW020138250726
13967UKWH00002B/732

9 781304 016850